The Love in Ve/Ains

JAYAN ASRANI

Made with ♥ on the Notion Press Platform

www.notionpress.com

Disclaimer

This book contains a parody of an existing song. This parody is created for entertainment purposes only and is not intended to infringe upon the original copyright holders' rights. The original song remain the property of their respective copyright owners. The parodied lyrics are not intended for commercial use or distribution.

About the Author

JAYAN ASRANI, Born in Kanpur, Uttar Pradesh, began to write poems at an amateur age of twelve. ‘THE LOVE IN VE/AINS' unveils the mirrors of being in love. One can always keep themselves in the shoes of the poet and read the writings as they, themselves are the main character who is being talked about.

Foreword

In the realm of poetry, a new voice emerges, tender and true. Jayan Asrani's debut collection, "The Love in Ve/ains", flows with the pulse of life, exploring the intricate networks of the human experience. With each turn of the page, Jayan's words will transport you through the veins of love, loss, and self-discovery.

"The Love in Ve/ains" is more than a collection of poems; it is a journey through the labyrinth of the soul. With a voice that is both hauntingly beautiful and profoundly relatable, Jayan Asrani beckons readers to pause, reflect, and find solace in the universality of their emotions. His debut work stands as a testament to the enduring power of poetry to heal, inspire, and transform.

Prepare to be moved, for "The Love in Ve/ains" is a testament to the resilience of the human spirit and the enduring power of poetic expression. Each poem is a glimpse into the depths of Jayan's heart, offering readers a chance to connect with their own inner worlds and discover the profound beauty that lies within.

Preface

"The Love in Veins" is a poetic odyssey that navigates the complex pathways of the human heart. Jayan Asrani's debut book explores the intersections of love, emotions, and the nervous system, revealing the beauty and vulnerability that lies within.

Through this collection, Jayan Asrani paints a vivid tapestry of human experience, each poem pulsating with life and authenticity. The verses invite readers to traverse the winding corridors of their own hearts, exploring the delicate balance between passion and pain, connection and isolation.

With a voice that resonates with both tenderness and strength, Jayan's poetry captures the essence of what it means to be human. His words serve as a mirror, reflecting our deepest desires, fears, and triumphs. "The Love in Veins" is not just a book of poems; it is a journey of self-discovery, a celebration of the emotional spectrum, and an exploration of the profound connections that bind us all.

Prepare to be moved by the raw honesty and lyrical beauty of Jayan Asrani's writing, as "The Love in Veins" takes you on an unforgettable journey through the depths of the human soul.

Prologue

In the rhythmic beat of veins, where love flows,
A tale of heartbeats, and soulful glows.
A journey begins, through verses true,
A poet's debut, with heart anew.

"The Love in Ve/ains" unfolds,
A tapestry rich, with emotions told.
Join me, dear reader, on this path I've trod,
And let the love within these pages, be your gentle lodestar.

Index

Enter without expectation,
Let the pages whisper secrets,
As you wander through the veins,
Of love, loss, and life's sweet retreats.
No map can guide you, no key can unlock,
The mysteries hidden within these blocks,

Only your heart, your soul, your deepest sighs,
Can navigate the twists and turns that lie.
Within the veins of love, where poetry resides,
A world of emotions, where heartbeats abide.
So, take your time, dear reader, linger and roam,
Let the words seep in, like a gentle, sweet perfume.

HERE IS A FLOWER FOR THE READER.

I'm a book,
Filled with a lot of stories,
Stories that maybe broken,
Or just reshaping into something.
Stories that are written with colours,
Colours that can't be seen...
Colours that no pen can write,
And these colours made me....

We fall for some or the other person in our lives. It's like many a times we kind of have a crush on someone, but there is a very less probability that this crush gets promoted into the love of our life. Maybe it's one sided, maybe both of them feel the same or maybe it's hurting for someone who had already suffered once when they got attached to someone.

Let's Get on the journey of the train carrying the loads of mixed emotions one feels during this time.

You know there are some people we just click with. We just start to feel that comfort with them from the very first time we meet them. These people are just amazing. The talks just click, the humour just hits and the vibes that match. But what if you fall in love with them? If they'll also love you, they will happily fall with you and will be there to pick you up too. But the problem arises when they do not love you back, you'll start to love them but no one would be there to pick you up because nothing comes easy to us and love definitely tops that list. We eventually meet those people, who are destined to us and something that is going to make all the difference is how hard we try and implement our efforts to make them stay. Love can be uncertain, it can be scary too. If two people are in love with each other and still they can't make it work, there's literally no problem in that because this word "love" doesn't have any rules so nobody knows how to be good at it. Every time it carries a different experience with it, and that's the only beauty this word love holds.

Moving on.

Two words that can turn you up into a whole different person. Sometimes it feels like hell while trying to move on because the overthinking and the memories strike even if you try to keep yourself busy. And when you experience it all for the first time, you really don't know how to react and how to surpass this feeling. The one person who knows all about how to make you happy isn't there to cheer you up and the one who always made you feel more important than their ego isn't even there to listen to you, they suddenly disappear and it's a really bad feeling.

At this stage you reach the point of life where you don't have any energy to talk or any stories to share. It is the time when you really miss yourself, you miss the one who was always excited about little things coming up in life. You miss everything about yourself but the thing you really want to forget is that version of yourself who was not prepared to see the things go upside down.

And like everything has pros and cons, this phase too carries some positives too. At a leisurely pace you learn to walk away from those memories, those feelings and that attachment. This is the time when you realise that, moving on hurts, but what hurts more is holding on to it. And the most beautiful thing that moving on carries is that you come up as becoming a whole new person who's stronger than the previous one.

You know there are some special people in our lives. The ones who laugh with us at our bad jokes, people who also stand with us in our tough times.

And one day they just leave. They said that they'll be there for you "always" know? Where are they now? I know it's hard, it's really hard, but don't you think that you still don't have any kind of grudges or any type of real anger issues with them.

They still have the right to knock the door of your life, and they'll find out that, the door was never really closed for them. And there is also a reason behind it, this is because when they said that they'll be there for you always, they actually meant it. Even if it was not a forever one, but just think of the small time they stayed, they didn't make you feel like you're the temporary one.

The joy of every moment felt like forever know?

And remember, when the time will be right, you'll find yourselves together with someone again, and hopefully this time always and forever will be always and forever...

Someone once asked me,
What's the power of a poem?
My heart whispered,
Whispered the secrets of a power unknown.

A power to convey a painful thought,
A power to help the one who has been through a lot,
A power to carry one's emotion's plot,
A power to empower the daunted for giving yet another shot.

Some intuitions which are bleeding,
Or some past that hurts,
Some really unimaginable feelings,
Which are sown and taped into words.

A poem flies,
Flies like beyond the universe is located its home.
It never dies,
Because perhaps, the universe is itself a poem...

“THE PULSING SOLITUDE AND THE UNSPOKEN LONGING”

He is the bright moon in the night,
And she is the sun who helps him shine him with it's light.
He wishes her scars to be in his heart,
And she wants to be the only one in his arms.
Thinking of what the other one would say,
They silently prioritised each other,
And both of them decided to stay...

Saw that flip of hair,
And those eyes with that deadly stare.
The personality and the vibe,
Was enough to make me high.
The smile was the next thing I fell for,
And there was nothing more I could ask of.
All I wanted was to just call her mine,
Don't know what's gonna happen,
But I've started to believe in love one more time...

He held her name on his tongue,
And she loved him inspite of every mistake he had done.
She literally looked in his eyes when he used to talk,
And his hands were always around her's when at the night they used to walk.

When the hug pressed their skins against each other,
And both the souls got the way to cure.
It was then they knew,
Another one was a missing part of them, That they were looking for.

Like The roads that join,
Like The seas that meet,
The two hearts met,
And made each other complete...

Those long tied hair,
Bound to be messed up.
And as the swirls fall down,
I feel those butterflies in my stomach.

The innocence between those spirals,
Is one of her two eyes.
Making me feel I could do anything for them,
So that they never carry those cries.

The love for those eyes,
The love I carry for her.
Makes my heart skip a beat,
I'm on a ride of a roller coaster.
The ride takes me to new heights,
Reaching there my soul making those flies.
Giving me a feel of being in some heaven,
And my love for her lands somewhere between those skies...

Words,
Can act like poison...
Yeah, words,
Can also be a potion...

Can be used to betray,
Can help to stand again...
Can be those who makes one's day,
Can act like salt on one's strain...

When unsaid,
It can kill you from the core,
If said,
They may have the power to hurt the other one more...

Sometimes saying them can be good too,
They may act like a gum for the broken pieces of one's heart...
Sometimes not saying them can be the best,
They may carry the the weight to save you from falling apart...

Words,
They have the power to carry one's emotions...
Yeah words,
They have the protection to save one from their erosion...

They have a freedom,
A freedom to roam.
And why not,
At last they helped me pour my thoughts into a poem...

If you block out,
I'll still be here.
If you want me,
I'll be all around and everywhere.

If you want to talk,
I'll always be marked to hear.
If you turn around,
You'll always find me standing there.

Can't get through any of those words,
That can make my perspective for you defined.
Can't gift you the whole world,
But will present you all of mine.

Wanna get us together,
Wanna make both of us being called as 'we',
Wanna make sure of the love I want to present,
Is the same love you feel,

Wanna say something only if agree,
Wanna bend on my knee,
Holding your hand, Saying it to thee,
That, In the future if by some miracle you ever find yourself in the position to fall in love again,
Fall in love with me.

If only I had known,
That you were afraid to say.
I would have allowed myself,
Would have had a way out for you to convey.

If only I had seen,
That you always wanted to confess.
I would have accepted it already,
Cause, you know I was always obsessed.

I would have held you tight,
Like you were more delicate than a flower.
Would have taken care of you like,
You are the only green left in my garden's grass.

I wouldn't have let you go,
If only I had known that this was going to end.
Would have hugged you so hard,
That would've felt like 'You were always more than a friend.'

What to say,
And what not to.
Can't really sense,
After catching myself near you.

Seeing you in front,
Makes my heart take giant pumps.
Every time I have you around,
Each butterfly inside me jumps.
Every cheesy thought I get,
it gets carried from dumps.

I am a lock,
Will you be the key?
I'm a river,
Will you be the sea?
I'm stuck in here,
Will you set me free?
If you'll say yes,
There's a thing I can guarantee,
Will always and always stand for thee,
Will hold the ring bending on my knee,
With a question of life that,
Will you marry me?

Well I'm clearly afraid of losing the bond,
So will stay away yards.
I know I'm falling in love,
And I know it would probably be hard.

Maybe I shouldn't confess it,
Maybe it's the idea I shall discard.
So you'll never get to know about it,
And I think this will be my only regard.

There was a promise that we made,
Will remain friends, decade after decade,
Won't fall for each other,
But things went outta my hands before this promise was even in the debate.

I hid my feelings then,
I'm hiding them now,
Will always be silent about them,
And confessing them won't be allowed.

But still,
If you allow me to express,
You would surely doubt yourself for days.
The love I don't talk about,
Is the love that can outgrow every feeling in each possible way.

I don't know,
How she was alone.
Selflessly hated by everyone,
Even the one's her own.

When I met her,
I saw a beautiful soul.
I saw a girl,
With scars making her a whole.

She heard everyone's pain and suffering,
She comforted them when their hearts were hurting.
But when things started tearing her heart off,
No one heard her even when her life was burning.

The moment I held her hand,
And saw her fist,
I was blown and stunned,
When I saw the scars of cuts in her wrist.

The day I saw this,
I made her a promise.
Will fill these wounds up,
Will fill up colours in her darkness.

I will stand for her,
Cause, she has been through my lowest.
I'd make up for everything,
Cause she has always been my closest.

The day will surely come,
When I'll fill up for all these pains.
Will make her the happiest,
So that she doesn't hide her tears in the rains.

And during all these rains,
I'd be the one holding her hand.
And when no one would do,
I'd be the one to understand.

You said I didn't understand your words,
But I never needed any words to love you.
You said my love was temporary,
But for me the meaning of love was only you...

All those words,
All that hate,
All these fights,
It was all our fate...

I wanted you always,
I was never ready for things to get this tough.
You missed me when to talk, you had no one,
But then too for you, I was never enough...

You broke me so much,
So much that this heart broke in millions.
Broke like every part carried a memory of you with it.
That's when I knew, to love someone till this extent,
It takes one heart in billions.

One sided love,
Let's define the three words above.
Making people see the emotions we carry,
Letting them know about purest form of love.

Lost in her beauty,
Most in those eyes.
Asking nothing more than her heart,
And to ask I have no words to prescribe.

The world might be crazy for her,
Or the universe might burn her dreams in fire.
I'll fight even with the gods for her life,
But still can't have despite wanting her being my only desire.

My silent eyes being speechless,
These lips trembling while I talk.
Her presence is enough for me,
Her talks are a medicine during that side street walk.

Meaning all those things I never said,
Loved her in all those dreams I always had.
Still didn't said a word to her,
Cause, she was the best thing I always had.

And now I'll leave silently,
Now I won't be there for her.
Stories of me and her would mark an end,
Will ruin this thing like a photo is disturbed blur.

But I can dedicate this whole life to her,
Cause, she gave me all those things to adore.
And being in love with her would hurt me though,
But not being in love with her would hurt me more.

What's one sided love?
One when falls in it,
There's nothing above.
And once you wear this glove,
You'll want to stop the winds,
But this would never be enough.

When there's no one to pick up,
Then why is it something that one falls in?
And when people have a doubt in the cup,
Then why is it something that one holds in?

Sometimes making us feel like a stranger,
And sometimes it feels like having a cuisine.
Who are you?
What do you actually mean?
Are you the red sign of the danger?
Or you carry the flags that are green?

Like a poetry, I don't know where you started,
But I know that the end would take up my love's infinity.
"Hey, one sided love" I can say that you are half hearted,
Because joining two hearts to one is only the word 'love's' dignity.

Yes, you're the last one for me,
The last one to be mine,
The last one with whom I'd dine,
The last one to make me feel loved,
The last one where no one's above.
The last one for whom I'm kind,
The last one to come and never leave my mind.
The last one after whom I'd be alone,
The last stop I'd call as my home.

“THE HEART’S LAMENT AND THE WEEPING VEINS”

Sitting here with no one,
Cause, I Don't wanna socialize.
Wanna be someone,
No one should recognize.

Scared of making friends,
Yes, it's me.
Cause everyone pretends,
So will thee.

Tired of being the temporary one,
Tired of being one of those last options.
Just need a break from everyone,
I'm sorry, I won't be able to stand upon your expectations.

Wanna be someone's priority,
Who will be my sole authority.
The one who could understand the sadness behind my smile,
The one who'd be ready to walk together just one more mile..

I still imagine you with me
In our favourite song.
I still stalk you,
Whenever I'm tired of being strong.

Cause I can't reach out to you now whenever I'm sad.
I don't even know how to say 'Hi',
Cause I know I messed up so bad.

Those words that I shouldn't have said,
Those thoughts that I shouldn't have expressed.
Yes it hurted,
The whole night I wasn't able to sleep.
It ended without any chaos,
But still made my eyes weep.

Anxious thoughts keep getting harder,
As the night keeps getting darker.
Staring at the moon while lying near that lake,
Slowly the sun begins to rise and I'm still awake.

I tried to block you out,
But found it far too loud.
Then I heard your voices in my head,
Filled with those words you never said.

One day we were meant to be together,
The other day meant to be apart.
Maybe I'll find someone who is better,
But you'll always be the one I would love from the bottom of my heart.

Will live with your memories,
Cause I have no other choice.
But when the heart will hurt,
I'll make these tears my voice.

You were my favourite,
And Still you are gone.
You were the only one I loved,
Yet I had to move on.

You were someone I could do anything for,
But I wasn't just strong enough to hold on.
It's been long since we've stopped talking,
Still I don't know how to forget you.
Carrying the same love, alone I'm walking,
Just want you to get me through.

Years passing like one and two,
All I want is to see the old you.
Who was always excited to talk to me,
Who's replies were always there at the count of three.

I did let you go,
I did accept this fate.
But my heart,
Whenever it thinks of you,
All it asks me, Is to just wait.

Sometimes I feel like I'm falling,
Why aren't you there to hold me?
Sometimes I feel like I'm all alone,
Was I so stupid to love thee?

I'm Smiling,
When all I want is to cry.
I'm Quite,
When all I want to shout and not to stay shy.

Believed in happy endings,
Saw the sad ones though.
But what name should be of this,
Where I can't decide whether to stay or go.

We had many more memories to store,
Maybe you weren't interested for it anymore,
Was dying to talk to you,
But now I just can't hold on more.

Silently will walk away,
And give our story the end.
Maybe I wasn't able to understand you,
Or maybe I was just not a good friend.

Yeah, I was dumb,
Now I am stunned.
The day I saw the truth,
Since the day I'm numb.

The love is in vain,
The tears are a stain.
I can feel the remains,
Of the heart which is in pain.

Thought I was your beloved,
When I saw the way you treated.
Everything dropped down the eyes between those rains,
The night I got to know that you cheated.

Weren't the words enough to say,
That you didn't love me back.
I wouldn't have asked you to stay,
I wouldn't have disturbed thee's track.

What's the point,
Of all this explanation after this play.
How can there be a solution now,
When I got to know everything this way.

If only I had known,
That it was our last conversation going through,
Maybe I would have got some extra texts to adore...

If only I had known,
That it was the last time which I'm spending with you,
Maybe I would have planned it for an hour more...

If only I had known,
That we won't be completing our promises which were due,
Maybe I would have already crowned them before...

If only I had known,
That we can't be the laces of one shoe,
Maybe I would have had the other part of the pair to store...

If only I had known,
That I'll regret this and will wish for things to renew,
Maybe you would have been here with everything cured.

If only I had known,
If only I had known...

Memories,
Something to think,
Something with mixed emotions,
Something more edible than ink.

Sometimes gets in the mind while lying,
Or maybe while having a glass of drink.
Can be the happiest,
Can make you feel sad too.
Can carry some hate for someone you love,
Can make some love for the one you hate too.

Overthinking them isn't the potion,
Start having a control over the burn.
Control that will carry an option,
Option which will find out a way for you to learn.

They'll teach you,
Teach you to move on,
They'll motivate you,
Motivate you by saying "C'mon!!!"

It's the time,
To carry the hope,
Of who I am,
Not who I was.

Distance or difference?
Does not matter,
Love or hate?
Carrying it together.

Wanted to gift you the rose,
That must've been found dry in your diary,
Wanted to give you the letters of love,
That would've described our bond's priori.

But now,
I let you go,
I let you flow.
You followed the crowd,
I'm choosing to grow.

Because, you didn't care,
For the tears that shed.
You didn't listen, The voices in that head.
You didn't see, The pain in those eyes.
You didn't feel, The love that cries.

To the one I gave all my love,
Wasn't it ample?
Giving you my whole world,
Was it any bad example?
I know I shouldn't have forced you to love,
But for me,
It was just you and no one above.

You really were the one in my mind,
You really were someone,
For whom my love was blind.

It's been so long since you are gone,
It has been too hard for me to move on.
Why am I stuck?
Why can't I get over you?
I just can't admit it,
But it's me who loves nobody but still you.

I saw the little changes,
I saw you go,
I am seeing you with them now,
I can't even ask," Why so?"
If I could have,
I'd have stopped you though,
But I saw it hidden in your eyes,
That you wanted me to let you go.
So I'll let it be,
And will let the things flow.
Will just wait here,
And will give my happiness another reason by seeing you grow.

I'll leave quietly,
I'll walk away.
I know it'll hurt you,
But maybe that's the only way.

You made me feel strong,
When I was at the lowest.
I don't really want to, but now,
It's not a good feeling, being your closest.

No I'm not in love with you,
And neither you've done anything to make me fall apart.
It would not be easy for us because,
Thinking about it only breaks my heart.

Let's accept this distance,
Let's accept the difference.
I don't know what I'm doing is right or not,
I really don't know what we'll leave as an instance.

THE THIRD PERSON

Whether it be friendship,
Whether it be love.
Whenever they enter,
The bond becomes the worst.

Those promises are now seen nowhere,
The care is being shown to the person there.
The talks aren't the same anymore,
The vibes do not match anymore.
It feels like there's only one investing time,
The other one does care no more.

Why am I blaming the third one,
Else the one who should be blamed is thee.
You only allowed them to interfere,
Now again the one left out alone is me...

Tears trace their path down my face,
Speaking the language of my heart's ache,
They threaten to erase my joy's embrace,
And now, our paths are bound to break.

We embraced for one last time,
Recalling the days when we used to dine,
Tears flow as we cherish the memories we've made,
All night, I replayed the moments of our dates.

As the tears coursed down my cheeks,
Thoughts of you always make me weak,
Sitting alone in a quiet corner, so bleak,
I've worn a multitude of smiles,
But in solitude, I weep.

Thoughts roaming in my mind,
Cause, I lost my home.
Gonna pour these thoughts,
Gonna give rise to a poem.

Don't know how to get started,
But still remember the first time we regarded.
Tears finding their way out through my eyes,
I think they got to know that our ways have been parted.

What went wrong?
Why're you gone?
Ain't able to figure out,
Can't tell myself to stay strong.

How will I reach out?
How will I handle these voices so loud?
Do you also miss me?
If yea then please help me escape this crowd.

How to express this feeling?
I only cried down kneeling.
We made each other so complete that whenever together,
My wounds would itself start healing.

I am currently in a state,
Where I am awake all night straight.
Thinking that no one's there to hear me now,
While listening to all those songs with which I can relate.

Being okay nowadays is something I pretend,
With no confidence my shoulders down and bend.
All I want is you and both of us to be complete,
And with this I would like to give this poem an end.

Unbraiding my feelings,
They're falling down as the drops.
I'm hating being me,
Cause all those memories just can't be cropped.

Yeah I was quiet,
Cause I was stunned.
All those things you said,
Made my heart stop and my body numb.

Those words echoed so loud in my ears,
That I made myself silent.
Tears just didn't come out at that time,
But the voices outside and inside me were just too violent.

Quietly was sitting in the park then,
Seeing those dry leaves fall.
Those leaves were just falling like my confidence,
Since you said those things and between us stood up a wall.

I would have proved myself,
I would have had you back again,
But you didn't show that trust in me,
So I decided to go through with this pain.

I was still standing in the midst,
It was a moment when my inner kid was actually killed.
When you left, it didn't change the world.
But you know what, my world did.

A day She'll realise how much I used to care,
She'll miss my irritating texts,
She'll remember that,
There was this guy who was always there.

One day everyone would leave and,
Everything will fall apart,
She'll read my old texts,
And would remember that this guy loved her from the bottom of his heart.

Always and always ignoring my texts,
Now it's me only whom I suspect.
Every time making me feel that I'm not sufficient,
Now I only feel like I'm not efficient.

Hating me all the time,
Was loving you such a big crime?
Breakup won't hurt,
Neither breaking of heart.
Once you fall for one sided love,
Your world would fall apart.

Your love won't be enough for them,
They'll take it for granted.
Believe me dear,
It's just a crop failure to the love seeds that you've planted.

Now I know,
You are not for me anymore.
I expected it,
my guts did,
That you want us to continue no more.

Why don't you come up to me,
To tell me that I ain't sufficient now?
Don't you remember how open we were to each other,
Then why don't you come and speak your heart out?

My lungs are feeling suffocated,
My chest is tight.
My body shivers,
Dizziness too is at it's all might.

Tears are falling, and no track of time,
Thinking, maybe we weren't deemed to be destined.
Sweat is flowing out through all my body,
And also, I feel, chills running down my spine.

If I ever find friendship in my heart again,
It will be only for you.
Cause my friend I used to consider thee as my home,
And mate, this soul will never stop searching for you.

I'm gonna leave this poem here,
I'm gonna leave it as "to be blended."
Because like most of the stories have,
Hopefully ours is still not ended.

Sometimes who wants to run,
Run to someone,
Who was the only one.

To someone who used to relate,
And when went there,
made a mistake,
A mistake that he found himself alone,
Got Trapped there,
with no way to escape.

He felt suffocated to go elsewhere,
Because when he tried to.
People outside weren't able to hear,
Cause obviously they didn't want to.

He always used to hear that,
"If not in this universe, Maybe in the other one though."
He too used to argue that,
"Why always in the other universe, Why not in this one I can show?"

He used to be a calm person,
Filled with emotions but was intact,
Filled with sadness but didn't react,
Filled with love which he didn't had.

An incomplete ending to this poem too,
An incomplete ending to HIS poem too,
Because when she left, she didn't bid him adieu,
Which again left him a hope that she'll come back to get him through.

Where would I might have gone?
Where would I might have cried?
Cuz when looked for it,
I only found the ruins of my safe place that just died.

Never before I had so many words to say,
So much that if in her shoes,
I would have been named as the one who had betrayed.

Maybe you wouldn't have loved me,
Loved me like I did,
But darling if you had trusted the love I carry,
The void from your side, my love alone would have filled.

But in the universe, if someone asks me about her,
I'd say that, there was this girl with me for once,
For once when I was blessed.
Oh to be loved by her, It's a feeling,
which I'd say is the best.
Her eyes carried the innocence,
The innocence which can never be expressed.
When with her, I used to be lost,
Lost somewhere, where I used to ignore the rest.
She felt like a home to me though,
A home where I was just a guest.

The dullness in me,
No confidence is seen.
Oh moon! In the night,
When falls the light,
In the light, a dark spot is to be seen,
And the one who lies there, yes, it's me.

A ray of light,
Or a beam of hope.
Oh moon you glow so much,
Still can't make me cope.

I heard you're an ethereal body,
I saw you as the one who glimmers.
But here I'm lying down,
Unable to receive your shimmers.

At the very next moment I closed my eyes,
Realising how silly I am to fight.
To fight with the resplendent moon itself,
The moon that doesn't even reflects its own light.

And when my pupils contracted at the dawn,
I saw that the moon and the sun intertwined.
A smile passed and the realisation hit again,
That the moon is nothing, but a state of mind.

A leaf falls,
Falls for the tree,
And the tree let it go,
The tree let it flee.

And here I am flying,
Flying somewhere you didn't blow.
Your thoughts follow me like the winds,
Forgetting that the tree was the one to let go.

Was in love even with each part of your roots,
Not only with the branch to avail.
Always heard people turning yellow when hurt,
And then I saw myself pale, leaving your trail.

One morning, someone brooming,
Will take me alongside my likes,
And then I'd be burning with the rest,
Hoping that my eyes are somehow left.

Do come with the winds looking for my glances,
And If you find them, do look into those pieces chopped.
You'll then realise that my eyes were carrying an ocean filled with emotions,
But I could only express a drop, my emotions cropped.

Tears in my eyes,
All this time I was hurt.
Knowing we'd never be the same again,
Came out a feeling of being alone in a desert.
You were a part of me,
No not even a part,
You were my whole heart,
A heart which is now torn apart.
Because it loved you like none,
And thought that you were the only one...

Sitting as the evening knocks
The last left rays of the sun.
The rays are slowly setting into the dusk,
Setting into the dark where I'm left out stunned.

It isn't the night,
It's actual dark.
No moon to be seen,
Not even a slight spark.

I can't stop.
I can't stand.
Am I stuck?
I can't land.

What's this state?
What's this stage?
What actually the choice is?
Of a mind full of voices.

READING FOR TOO LONG?

TAKE A TEA BREAK!

OHH, I SEE! YOU ARE NOT FOND OF TEA.

HERE'S SOME COFFEE FOR YOU!

"TWO PART POEMS."

THE LAST GOODBYE

As the things didn't work out,
I came back to the moment we met...
With those scars all around,
I saw the boundaries that we never really set...
Don't you think that ending this was tough?
Don't you think that the last goodbye wasn't enough?

Together we had grown,
Those cherishing memories we had sown...
We were then together,
With a feeling of being forever...
There are only these nights left out to roam,
Roaming and thinking,
How can we even say goodbye to our home?

Yeah I remember the time,
When you saw me losing my spark...
You were there for me,
You really saved me from getting lost in the dark...
Yeah you were there,
But where are you now...
Can't you see me getting into the past again,
You only made yourself distant somehow...

I wanted to talk,
But you didn't really understand...
When I wanted you here,
You weren't there for me to stand...
You could've also asked if I'm fine,
Now you're making my insecurities the reason behind our decline...
I have nothing more left to justify,
So I ended up the things,
And gave it a name as,"The Last Goodbye."

I LOVE YOU, BUT

vs

BUT, I LOVE YOU

I love you, But,

Some days I Just wanna get some time for me,
So, these times I cannot be there to stand for thee.
Some days I am just too cold to only talk out,
Maybe I feel like giving my heart a habit of blocking people out.
I won't always be there to listen to you or hold your hand,
And for all this what I wanna say is,
I hope you understand.

But, I love you,

Because at the end of the day I only have you who'd ask me if I was fine,
And, you trust me that I'll be available if you need me anytime.
Sometimes I'll just sit beside you saying nothing,
I'll make myself relax with you cause you are my comfort ring.
Sometimes you'll also feel low and won't have anything to say,
But as I said,
I'll always choose to stay,
I'll just listen to your silence,
Will be there to hold your hand,
And, you don't have to worry, Because, I do understand...

THE FRIENDSHIP GAME

Oh hi, what's your name?
The talks came.
Omg our hobbies are same.
The bond became.

From, I've to go Papa has came,
To talking hours and hours at night
On the topics that were lame.

We'd spend nights conversing,
oh, how we'd ignite,
On topics seemingly mundane,
under the moonlight.

Bitching about others,
playing those tricky mind games,
We declared ourselves best friends,
But now it's not the same.
I can't place all the blame,
But it's a pity," Who's he, I don't even know his name."
You now exclaim.

From cherishing those moments,
To never crossing paths again,
From chatting endlessly,
To no more messaging to sustain.

From laughing for hours on end to end,
To forcing a smile when memories flood the brain,
But now you're attempting to return,
After throwing me like an old cloth with strains.

This time,
I don't wish for us to become the same,
Recalling the past,
I'm allowing karma to play its game.

“THE HARMONY OF MEMORIES”

Someone has said it right that," We don't feel sad for the one's who has left the world behind. We feel sad for those who in this world are left behind. You know when the god calls, we just can't hold on to people, seriously we can't, because the only superpower that people believe in is itself the god. He created us, he'll destroy us, He created everything around us, he'll himself destroy everything around us. And we really can't do anything about it. At this time people tell us to accept it and let go, but is it really that easy? Will they tell themselves the same thing when they'll be going through the same pain?

The answer to both the questions is a big 'No' because -

First of all, we just can't accept it that they've left us and all of this feels like a bad dream. The moments spent with that person, places you've been to together, had a fight with them, the way they shadowed their love towards you, or let it be whatever you think of that person, by just remembering all this we ourselves are holding us back from being happy.

And the people who stay with us all this time and ask us to let go, I know they'll not say themselves the same thing while going through the same but you know they just want you to remember that this isn't the end, because you're also an important part of universe, an important part of god's plan and your life matters too. So give yourselves some time, you're going to make through this, make through every little or big thing that comes to break you. I know this might seem easy to say and hard to feel but believe me once you try and understand them, it won't be just words. Just put your faith on God and the rest will be taken care by him.

You'll get a call,
You'll rush for cab,
Yeah that'd be all,
When I'll be on bed,
my condition going bad.

Just a few more breaths would be there go,
Will be going through the last of those beats.
That's when I'll let you know,
That you were the reason why my heart used to beat.

Just made an assumption that you'll be there by my bed,
Will you be?
If yes, we'll talk about all the memories we've made together,
But my friend, don't you weep.

We'll smile,
We'll talk about when I'll be in those stars,
We'll welcome the moments of silence,
When drops would fall from those going to close scars.

And then I'll ask you to let me keep my head on your lap,
I'll just look into your eyes calling out your name.
And then you'll rub your fingers down my hairs,
That's when I'll close my eyes, never to be opened again.

You came like a dream,
Gave me unicorns when I was okay with heirs.
But things always don't work as good as they seem,
God then taught me that dreams can also be nightmares.

Cried cats and dogs,
Tears drizzled down the cheeks like heavy raindrops.
Remembering that I used to wail sobbing,
When having a life without you just lied in those thoughts.

Seeing you lie pale in front of me,
Out came a feeling of being in a jail while I set you free.
Having one of the four shivery pairs while lifting your coffin,
Mine were literally the weakest among the rest of three.

You were my personal space,
Now whom will I call as my own.
When for the last time I'm now seeing your face,
I'm not ready to bid a goodbye to my home.

I'll fight with the gods itself,
I just want you back as a boon.
Would be really happy to lose the battle too,
At least we'll see each other on the other side soon!!!

Oh for those lonely nights,
Yeah for that overthinking of your mind.
You suffering from mental health,
Being yourself outside with no inner strength.
You tried to speak your heart out,
But people found it far too loud.
Ohh now they want you in their life again,
Seeking sorry for the mistakes they've previously made.
Now they say,
You'd have talked to them so they'd have tried to heal your scars.
And when you really did,
They started to turn out more and more harsh.
They're really ashamed cause,
Now you're in the stars, and six feets never felt so far...

Tonight,

I stepped inside, knocking the door of a memory where you live for me. As you saw me, you hugged me like those old days. Started chatting as we did previously. We chatted, bitched and did a lot of things together. But at the same time, it made me realize that it was just a memory and within a span of seconds my happiness turned into sadness and my laughter into tears.

Memories hit really hard to your heart,
To the broken pieces that were once torn apart.

They just come in our head, making our anxiety kiss our consciousness.
These memories sneaking out of my eyes and rolling down my cheek,
I saw them leaving me to myself now,
I don't know how I will live being so weak...

WRITER WANTS TO SEND YOU
VIRTUAL HUGS

"VEINS OF RENEWAL AND THE RHYTHM OF REDISCOVERY"

While walking on the new tracks of life,
I saw some of those old trains.
While searching for some new drops,
I met with some nostalgic rains.

Sitting in my room,
Far from everyone.
I am tired,
And want to talk to no one.

It's the day when my,
Hands are cold
And I am not able to speak,
No not because of the winters,
But it is my heart being so weak.

I'm becoming everything,
I don't want to.
I am becoming the one,
No one wants to talk to.

What's all in my mind,
Was a break.
Which at the very next moment,
I decided to take.

Suffering alone with my pain,
Hearing the drops pouring down of rain,
Went out to feel the water which washed me then,
And gave me a hope to try again.

Treehouse on the tree,
On the banks that quietly flowing sea.
Being with my own one,
It'll be me making myself free.

On a branch I saw a nest,
With a little life who was taking rest.
In the same sky we were the only two,
With different lives,
We were unbound too.

Carrying an ocean in my eyes,
In which I was swimming through.
A salty welcome to my on the loose life,
I was a bit of scared too.

When I saw the life marking attendance,
I once again marked myself present.
Screaming with the voice of my independence,
I saw my world becoming pleasant.

To all the sadness I was holding,
I went through it in a glance.
And when the time was unfolding,
I gave myself a second chance.

Its okay to fall down,
Its okay to not feel strong,
Its okay to drown,
Its okay to be the one who's wrong.
Its okay to feel low,
Its okay to fall apart,
Its okay to not follow the flow,
Its okay to not be the one who acts hard.
Its okay to think about what's wrong while you lay,
Its okay to have a thought on your life while you're awake.
You're a part,
A part that isn't fake,
A part of God's plan,
A part that is unimaginably great.

Every wave of life,
That taught me to live,
That helped me thrive,
And each one gave my life a thrill.

A wave that never made me regret,
Of being too much.
The other one never made me feel insecure,
Of not being enough.

A wave that helped me discover my depths.
The upcoming took me deep inside them,
So that I could fight Until the last of my breaths.

One by one these came and became a mantra for life,
Soothing every wound.
One came to cure,
And one came to protect the surround...

I choose not to speak,
I ask myself not to address,
I learn how no one understands,
I tell myself not to express.

Yeah, I did open up,
But only to my 2-3 friends.
It didn't work out too well,
I realized how everyone pretends.

Now my heart won't express things,
My mind will accept things.
I'll keep them to myself,
And learn to carry these strings.

But when the load will get too heavy,
And the control would be lost,
Shivers and tears will come,
Because I'd the only one left out to pay the cost...

Inside us there are some voices,
Which can't be heard.
Some words,
That aren't referred.
Some happiness,
That isn't known.
Some sadness,
Which isn't shown.
Some feelings,
That cannot be expressed.
Some warmth,
That now needs some rest.

There is a part of love inside us,
That is somewhere saved for later.
We deal with some poems inside us,
Whose weight can't be carried on by a paper..

Sometimes happy,
Sometimes sad,
But when you see through it,
Life isn't so bad.
Sometimes lost,
Sometimes found,
Come on,
it's your life,
You need to stick around.

Understand it in a musical way,
Be humble while playing the high notes of your life.
Remember not to fade out,
Even when you hit the lowest notes in the strife.
Sometimes it'll be the stream of water,
Sometimes it'd freeze like an ice,
Just follow this flow man,
And the sun will automatically begin to rise.

“MISCELLANEOUS”

There's music all around,
It is the only love,
With a rhythmic sound.

Headphones are on,
The level of volume is at max.
Outside world is just an illusion,
That is how hard the music impacts.

It calms my mind,
And makes me feel no pressure.
If found the right one,
Listening to it is such a pleasure.

Singing with the song,
I don't mind shouting the lyrics wrong.
It is something that makes me feel strong.

It felt right to me,
Yes, I love this,
Of course it is no shame.
And whenever felt like a moment off,
I turn on the music all over again....

One day,
On those cold nights,
I'll step out.
On a warm Sunday,
Wander here and there with no doubt.

One day,
I'll make it a routine,
I'll travel alone.
About those holidays in between,
Will visit a place where there is no one known.

Enjoying the foods of different places,
Seeing the lifestyle of the people having different phases.
I'll leave my footprints behind,
Maybe someone will one day follow those traces.

Drinking tea,
On the banks of sea.
It will be me,
Unlocking my freedom key.

I'll make travelling a routine,
I will step out,
Whether the day is cold or might the night be hotter.
I will wander, Whether the night is a cold one or a noon might be warmer.

It's the silence,
That got me here.
It's the stillness,
That I ended up being there.

Love here can't be described,
I learnt to love me back.
Life here can be combined,
I got the hope to start a fresh.

Yeah I'm lost,
Somewhere in those clouds,
Somewhere in those rains.
Can be found,
Somewhere away from the louds,
Somewhere between those mountains...

THANK YOU FOR READING!

HERE YOU GO!

LIKED THE GIFT?

So, once I tried writing a parody of the song 'Perfect' by Ed Sheeran. It goes like-

I got no one,
Except thee.
You know what I dream is that,
It ends as you with me.
Well, I love this girl,
And it's the same way she feels.
You know I'll never ever give up,
On you and me.

Cause we were just kids,
When we fell in love,
Not knowing what it was,
I will not give you up this time.

And darling, when you'll feel low,
I'll be there, you must know,
Hold my hand and I'll make you alright.

Baby I'm dancing in the dark,
With you between my arms,
Barefoot on the grass,
We're listening to our favourite song.

I'll there in your ups and downs,
Available for you all around,
Cause 'You're the one' and,
Darling, you are perfect tonight.

Epilogue

"And so, dear reader,
we reach the end,
Of this journey through love's tangled threads.
May the words that bled from my heart to yours,
Find a home in your soul, where love endures.

For in the veins of love, we find our truth,
A labyrinth of emotions, where heartbeats youth.
Though the path winds on, and the journey's long,
In love's embrace, we find our sweetest song."

THANK YOUUUUUUUU!!!!

www.ingramcontent.com/pod-product-compliance
Lightning Source LLC
LaVergne TN
LVHW041119150826
845673LV00007B/2126
* 9 7 9 8 8 9 6 3 2 6 0 1 4 *